MAKE YOUR OWN
WEATHER VANE

BY CHRISTOPHER HARBO

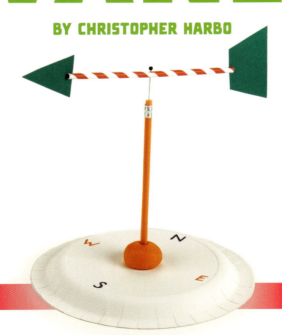

PEBBLE
a capstone imprint

Published by Pebble, an imprint of Capstone
1710 Roe Crest Drive, North Mankato, Minnesota 56003
capstonepub.com

Copyright © 2026 by Capstone. All rights reserved. No part of this publication may be reproduced in whole or in part, or stored in a retrieval system, or transmitted in any form or by any means, electronic, mechanical, photocopying, recording, or otherwise, without written permission of the publisher.

Library of Congress Cataloging-in-Publication Data is available on the Library of Congress website.
ISBN: 9798875225338 (hardcover)
ISBN: 9798875225048 (paperback)
ISBN: 9798875225291 (ebook PDF)

Summary: Make a simple tool to find out what direction the wind is blowing! Gather simple supplies and follow the easy steps to make your own weather vane.

Editorial Credits
Editor: Erika L. Shores; Designer: Heidi Thompson; Media Researcher: Jo Miller; Production Specialist: Tori Abraham

Image Credits
Capstone: Karon Dubke: all project photos, supplies; Shutterstock: ChiccoDodiFC, 5

The publisher and the author shall not be liable for any damages allegedly arising from the information in this book, and they specifically disclaim any liability from the use or application of any of the contents of this book.

Any additional websites and resources referenced in this book are not maintained, authorized, or sponsored by Capstone. All product and company names are trademarks™ or registered® trademarks of their respective holders.

Printed and bound in China. 6274

TABLE OF CONTENTS

Wonderful Weather Vanes 4

What You Need 6

What You Do 8

Take It Further 20

Behind the Science 22

Glossary 24

About the Author 24

Words in **BOLD** are in the glossary.

WONDERFUL WEATHER VANES

Weather vanes have been used for thousands of years. Often shaped like arrows, these simple science tools have just one job. They tell people which direction the wind is coming from. Follow the steps to make your own wonderful weather vane!

WHAT YOU NEED

- sturdy paper plate
- markers
- construction paper
- ruler
- scissors
- straight straw
- modeling clay
- pencil with eraser
- stick pin
- an adult helper

7

WHAT YOU DO

STEP 1

Turn the paper plate upside down.

Write the letters N, E, S and W around the edge of the plate. The letters should be written in that order while moving clockwise around the plate. They stand for north, east, south, and west.

STEP 2

Draw a triangle on a piece of construction paper. Make the triangle about 3 inches (8 centimeters) wide at the base and about 4 inches (10 cm) tall.

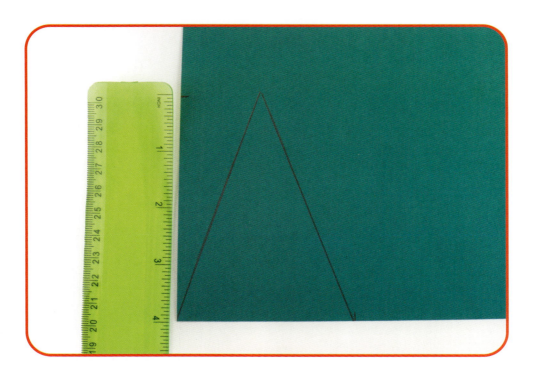

Cut out the triangle. Then cut off the top part of the triangle to create a small triangle and a large **trapezoid**.

STEP 3

Cut two slits into each end of the straw.

Slide the small triangle into the slits on one end of the straw. This is your arrow's tip.

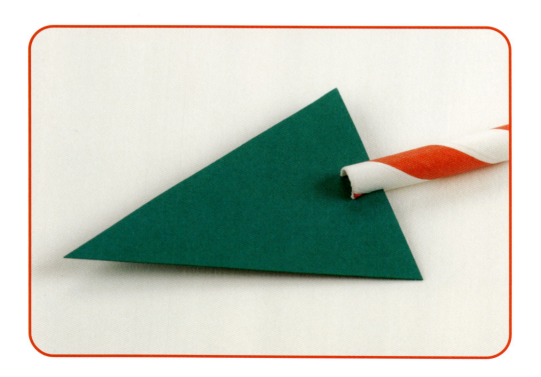

Slide the large trapezoid into the slits on the other end of the straw. This is your arrow's tail.

STEP 4

Form the modeling clay into a ball. Stick the clay ball in the center of the upside-down plate.

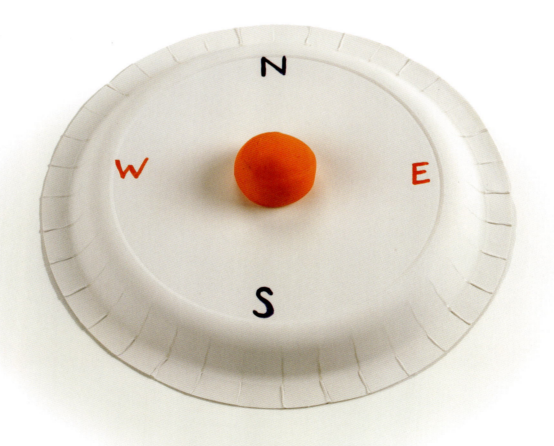

Push the pencil's point into the center of the clay ball so the pencil stands upright.

STEP 5

Push a stick pin through the center of the arrow's **shaft** and into the pencil's eraser.

STEP 6

Take your weather vane outside. Ask an adult to position the paper plate so its letters line up with north, south, east, and west.

Watch the arrow turn. Which direction is the wind coming from today?

TAKE IT FURTHER

Make your weather vane more **accurate** by adding more directions. Add NW for northwest between the W and the N. Add SE for southeast between the S and the E. Add NE and SW too.

Watch your weather vane for a week. Which direction does the wind blow from the most?

BEHIND THE SCIENCE

Weather vanes work by catching the wind. As the wind blows, it pushes against the arrow's wide tail. This **force** causes the arrow to **pivot** on the pin. The arrow stops when it points directly into the wind. Its tip tells you which direction the wind is coming from.

GLOSSARY

accurate (AK-yuh-ruht)—exactly correct

force (FORS)—any action that changes the movement of an object

pivot (PIV-uht)—to turn on a point

shaft (SHAFT)—the long, narrow rod of an arrow

trapezoid (TRAP-uh-zoid)—a four-sided shape that only has one set of parallel sides

ABOUT THE AUTHOR

Christopher Harbo is a children's book editor from Minnesota who loves reading and writing. During his career, he has helped publish countless fiction and nonfiction books—and has even written a few too. His favorite nonfiction topics include science and history. His favorite fiction books feature superheroes, adventurers, and space aliens.